woman.

A Celebration to Benefit the Ms. Foundation for Women

Essays by Carol Gilligan, Byllye Avery,
Wilma Mankiller, and Letty Cottin Pogrebin

Foreword by Marie C. Wilson
President of the Ms. Foundation for Women

RUNNING PRESS
PHILADELPHIA · LONDON

Foreword and Essays © 2000 by Ms. Foundation for Women
Photographs © 2000 by Magnum Photos, Inc

9   8   7   6   5   4   3   2   1
Digit on the right indicates the number of this printing

Library of Congress Cataloging-in-Publication Number 00-132686
ISBN 0-7624-0356-X

Picture research by Susan Oyama
Cover and interior design by Frances J. Soo Ping Chow
Edited by Patricia Aitken Smith
Typography: Goudy and Perpetua

This book may be ordered by mail from the publisher.
Please include $2.50 for postage and handling.
But try your bookstore first!

Running Press Book Publishers
125 South Twenty-second Street
Philadelphia, Pennsylvania 19103-4399

Visit us on the web!
www.runningpress.com

PHOTOGRAPHY CREDITS

1

ACKNOWLEDGEMENTS

Woman. would not have been possible without the hard work and dedication of many women. First, I would like to give special thanks to Byllye Avery, Carol Gilligan, Letty Cottin Pogrebin, and Wilma Mankiller for donating their time, talent, and wisdom to this book. I would also like to acknowledge the staff at the Ms. Foundation for Women who devoted long hours to this project's completion: Judy K. Evans, Elizabeth Coit, and Margaret LeMay. And finally, many thanks go to Patty Smith, our editor, who guided us every step of the way.

MARIE C. WILSON

President, Ms. Foundation for Women

1. Naomi and Isaac swim in Lambton County, Ontario, Canada. (1996)

FOREWORD

ALL MY LIFE, I HAVE LOOKED closely at pictures of females for the stories they could tell me. Looking at them, listening to their whispered secrets, helped me make sense of my own life and determine the kind of woman I wanted to be. They offered me courage, hope, and inspiration.

I was, in a sense, seeking what author Carolyn Heilbrun calls "stories to live by." In *Writing a Woman's Life*, she says, "We can only retell and live by the stories we have read or heard. . . . Whatever their form or medium, these stories have formed us all; they are what we must use to make new fictions, new narratives."

As a young girl in Georgia, pictures of women and girls fascinated me. In my favorite movies, girls rode horses, exhibited compassion and courage, flew over the rainbow, and ventured into issues of race and class with an openness and honesty that only girls have. Their grown-up counterparts danced, sang, went from rags to riches and changed their lives for the better. It was, after all, post–World War II—and in America, anything could happen.

As a young woman whose family was moving up from poor to a respectable working class, the opportunities these images presented made movement in my life seem possible. They offered me a passport to my future, a chance to transform my circumstances.

During my young adulthood, lived out at the height of the Civil Rights movement, photographs captivated me. I looked into the faces of African-American girls, their mothers and grandmothers, and saw lives that hadn't appeared on my movie screen. I sought out photos, examining them closely to understand how women who had been so poorly treated could still have smile lines. Perhaps they lived by the words of Harriet Tubman, who said, "What don't kill me makes me strong."

In early midlife, I attended the Third World Conference on Women in Nairobi. I saw women whose faces were hidden by veils, and Masai women who proudly displayed neck jewelry signifying rituals of circumcision. I saw women from places in the world where oppression made their work a daily risk. Their faces and bodies, like their voices, were chiseled by courageous acts.

I wanted photos of them all to lend me strength. I needed these photos because they told me, in the words of lesbian writer Judy Grahn, "Here is another way for women to be."

For countless women like me, the photographs contained within these pages—pictures of women in all stages of life—hold the promise of new scripts. Each image shows me another way for women to be, exemplifying the spirit of the work I do everyday with the Ms. Foundation for Women. In a world where women are hungering for other stories, I am proud to be a part of an organization that is crafting new possibilities for women and girls to take charge of and transform their lives. The women we have funded for years, the unsung and often unrecognized architects of a movement that has changed women's—and men's—lives for the better, have made new tales for our daughters and sons to live by. I would like to dedicate this book to women of all ages whose courage, leadership, and perseverance gives life to the stories behind their images.

MARIE C. WILSON

President, Ms. Foundation for Women

childhood

ESSAY BY CAROL GILLIGAN

2. A young girl sits at a table and writes in Paris, France. (1992)

GIRLS—WILD, EMOTIONALLY INTREPID, funny, astute, serious, gentle—are an inspiration for women writers. The eleven-year-old girl is the truth teller; she is irresistible. Her open face, her unflinching gaze, and her honest voice rivet novelists, filmmakers, and photographers. We forget this girl, covering her with idealized images or memories of childhood that are afterthoughts, superimposed on a reality of girlhood that is at once more complicated and simpler—an open-shuttered look at human possibility that tells a story we find painful to hear. Because girls remind us of who we have been, they reveal the real weather of human emotions and narrate a passage that we often do not remember: our initiation into a patriarchal world. Their resistance to the structure of our male-centric society captivates me. These girls take me back to a lost time of my youth.

I remember walking around the second-story ledge of a house with my friend Marianne. I recall swimming out into the waves with my father. I think of the world of girls fracturing at the time of adolescence into who was and who wasn't liked by the boys. I remember beginning to look at my looks, staring into a mirror and comparing my face with the faces that stared back at me from the pages of magazines—the way I looked and the way I thought I needed to look to be seen or looked at or loved in the world. I became a good girl on the outside, a bad girl on the inside, and then I turned myself inside out. I recollect talking about my mother, learning to look at her the way I had come to look at myself.

"But was it really like that?" Toni Morrison's narrator asks at the beginning of her coming-of-age novel, *The Bluest Eye*. She had drawn a picture of her childhood—the house old and cold, her mother harsh and impatient. It was a familiar image: a childhood lived in poverty, and her mother was harried, overburdened, and angry. She had split her love from her anger, so that love became idealized and anger the reality. And then, she remembered: "Love, thick and dark as Alaga syrup . . . I could smell it—taste it—sweet, musty, with an edge of wintergreen in its base—everywhere in that house." She remembered a mother who was present, who spoke all her feelings, the hands-on mother of her childhood, not an idealized image, "somebody with hands who does not want me to die."

As a culture, we have been captivated by stories of loss—a tragic story of lost childhood, lost innocence, lost love. I discovered in working with girls that what was in danger of being lost was often not innocence but knowledge. For Maxine Hong Kingston, it was "child sight" that disappeared: "now colors are fewer and gentler; smells are antiseptic." But she finds that the "throat pain" of childhood "always returns . . . unless I tell what I think." Jamaica Kincaid, in *Annie John*, shows how one story about childhood comes to cover another; the story she initially tells at age ten—a sensuous, vivid, emotionally accurate rendering of her life and her experience with her mother—becomes, by age seventeen, a familiar story about hypocrisy and betrayal: "So now I, too, have hypocrisy, and breasts (small ones), and hair growing in the appropriate places, and sharp eyes, and I have made a vow never to be fooled again."

Images of girls doing karate, swinging hula hoops, hugging dolls, driving, riding, dressing-up, hoeing, delighting in a bath in the sink, standing sadly in a doorway, brushing hair, studying alone, together, arms wrapped around fathers, nestling close to mothers, dancing with boys, trick or treating with one another—the smiling face of the girl in the black-hooded jacket, the astoundingly beautiful sad faces and arresting eyes of girls, the toddler who outrageously and unselfconsciously lifts her dress; the shyness of girls, the boldness of girls, swinging, teetering on the edge of womanhood. These photographs are a call to memory and a summons to think about the future of girls, the next generation of women.

I imagine a world in which girls' spirits flourish. It was when I began working with girls that I felt again the pleasure of moving freely in a girl's body and heard again the sound of a voice that broke free from second thoughts and instant revisions—my voice at the age of twelve. In *The Company of Women*, an all-women's Shakespeare troupe that Kristin Linklater and I co-directed, girls were the inspiration for women to speak freely and to know what we know. The spirit of girlhood returned, allowing true collaboration among women—a collaboration based on being truly present with ourselves and one another. The presence of girls can rapidly dispel what Toni Morrison's Claudia calls "fraudulent love."

The photographs here capture the variety of girls' inner worlds; from their expressions, we see their engagement. I long to hear their voices; I find myself giving them voices, looking at the photographs. It is enchanting to listen to their open-mouthed laughter, the belly-laughter of childhood, to remember the moment of wishing, with the birthday girl, inner thoughts racing, or to join in the game of double-dutch with the girls on the street.

The girl clutching her mother's skirt, looking directly at the gun, reminds us that girls' seeing includes seeing war, seeing suffering, experiencing violence, knowing violation. When I was working with girls, I was astonished to discover how often during the day girls are asked not to see what they see, or to say what they know.

Girls live in our world and we live in theirs. In entering girls' worlds, I discovered how powerfully I was called by girls. In Women Teaching Girls/Girls Teaching Women retreats, I saw teachers, mothers, therapists, and principals brought back to themselves and their passion in ways that became a call to act on behalf of girls' lives, and girls' brilliance, girls' health and girls' education. Women were confronting girls' resistance, remembering their own courage, taking steps to change the world—supporting girls' education, girls' health, girls' safety, girls' participation in the arts, in sports, in creative and critical thinking. These photographs bring me back to the years I spent in the company of girls and women—running on the beach with girls, listening to girls reading from their journals, going to museums with girls, seeing the world through girls' eyes, hearing girls sound and resound the human world, I remember . . . girlhood.

3. A newborn reaches out to touch her mother's face. (1965)

4. A schoolgirl giggles in Italy. (1998)

3

4

5

5. A young girl admires the flowers that she has picked. (1992)

6. In Paris, France, a toddler lifts her skirt to show off for the young man sitting next to her. (1982)

7. Two girls ride on the street. (1991)

6

8. A young girl hugs her father. (1956)
9. A birthday girl contemplates her wish before blowing out the candles on her cake. (1992)
10. A child races up the beach. (1996)

11. Children jump rope at a Police Athletic League event in New York City. (1981)

12. A girl swings a hula hoop in front of a shop. (1958)

13. Secrets are shared at a slumber party. (1996)
14. Two girls wear costumes for Halloween in Oakland, California. (1986)
15. Neighborhood children take turns pulling each other in a wagon. (1968)

13

14

16

17

18

16. Schoolgirls wear their uniforms and hats on the island of Jamaica.

17. Three girls laugh in the front row of a crowded movie theater.

18. A young girl holds a baby in Turkey. (1991)

20

19. A young girl sings in a recital for her class. (1950)

20. At a school run by the Mohammadiya movement, an orthodox practice of Islam,
   the school uniform covers the girls' head but leaves their legs bare. (1989)

21. A young student uses a computer. (1998)

21

22. The Once School for blind children in Seville, Spain, is an all-curriculum school. (1998)
23. A young girl kisses her mother goodbye before she boards the bus that will take her to elementary school twenty miles away. (1991)

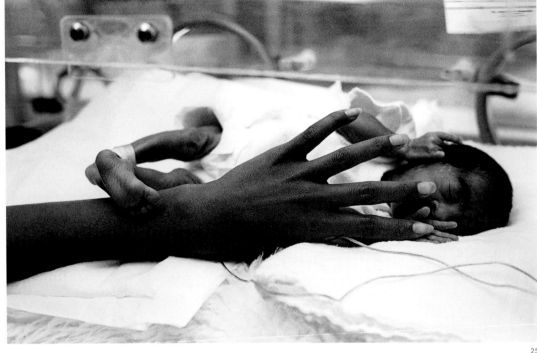

24. An Appalachian girl in Kentucky suffers from anemia and may die soon. (1996)

25. A mother gently touches her premature baby girl in the maternity ward at St. Joseph's hospital in Phoenix, Arizona. (1980)

26

27

26. Girls gather before making their first communion in Wales. (1980)

27. A young girl and her family light candles in worship at the Ayia Napa church in Limassol, Cyprus. (1993)

28. A Pongala girl dresses up for a festival at the temple in Trivandrum, Kerala, India. (1994)

31

32

29. A Kayapo Indian girl decorates her face for the Bemp Festival in Brazil. (1984)

30. These young Legong dancers perform a ceremonial dance after the cremation of King Ubud in Bali. (1979)

31. Mennonite sisters from Nuevo Ideal, Durango, Mexico, work in the seasonal labor market, planting and harvesting vegetable farms. (1994)

32. A snake charmer wears her newly caught cobra in India. (1989)

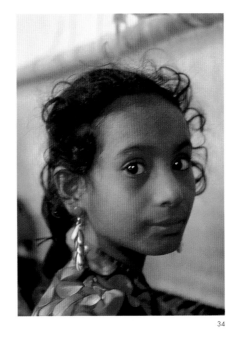

34

35

33. A young girl helps her father dig up mud to make
    adobe bricks in Agua San Tenango, Chiapas, Mexico. (1994)
34. This child of Bangladesh immigrants makes carpets for
    ten hours a day in Karachi, Pakistan. (1996)
35. Moslem refugees from Srebrenica sleep at the Tuzla airport
    in Bosnia. (1995)

36. A child stands behind a British Army crowd control line, watching the events after a bomb explosion in Belfast, Ireland. (1972)

37. In spite of Russian attempts to crush their declaration of independence from Moscow, traditional Chechens defiantly dance on the road, during the Chechnya War. (1996)

38

38. Children play in the streets of Belfast, Ireland. (1978)
39. A young girl straddles a stair rail and basks in the sun in Bronx, New York. (1995)
40. A girl swings at a playground in Barcelona, Spain. (1959)

41. Dancers practice at a ballet school in Russia. (1958)

42. Training an eight-year-old at the Seido Karate for Kids with Disabilities in New York. (1994)

41

42

44

43. A young girl stands on a fire escape in her underwear to cool off from the summer heat in New York City. (1966)

44. A mother and grandmother hold the hands of a toddling girl. (pre-1954)

adolescence

ESSAY BY BYLLYE AVERY

45. A war refugee in Afghanistan. (1985)

ADOLESCENCE—ONE OF THE MOST BEAUTIFUL and difficult times in a woman's life—is celebrated in countless Hollywood movies, television shows, and books. Coming of age—and all of the rites of passage that entails—endlessly fascinates because it is the defining time when adolescents discover and define who they want to be as adults. Growing up requires the exploration of many firsts—the first date, the first kiss, the first love, and the first heartbreak.

During this pubescent transition from girl to woman, a young woman learns about her world and tries to make sense of it all. She experiences her first menstruation and burgeoning sexuality. She struggles with issues of defining self-image, trying to understand what is beautiful and what it means to be a woman. She strives to gain knowledge about her role in the world around her.

She may experiment with many things—including sex, drugs, and alcohol. She will probably have to confront peer pressure to conform to societal ideals. She may explore the worlds of athletics or books—or she may not. But, all of these young women will face their dreams and hopes—and try to balance them with the expectations of parents, family, and friends.

In the following pages, young women are featured from all walks of life. They are athletes, gang members, students, unwed mothers, ballet dancers, young brides, war refugees, anorexics, soldiers, daughters, sisters, friends, and more. All of these adolescents have something in common. Young women from every socio-economic, racial, religious, or national background—all face the difficulty and beauty of coming of age. Their bodies are growing and changing into a woman's body with the consequent hormonal surges and mood swings. All must figure out who they want to be as women.

Some will easily determine who they want to be while others will struggle with the formation of their identity. Some will lead healthy lives while others will be struck with the difficulties of debilitating illnesses, poverty, or addictions. Still others will not conform to societal expectations while some will blindly follow the wishes of their parents, families, and friends. Some will be sexually attracted to men and some will be attracted to women. A number will lose their virginity early on while others will wait for marriage to have sex. Some will pursue education while others will drop out of school. Many will care more about their friends than their family, while others will put their family first. Most will think that they are too fat, a few will think that they are too skinny, and some won't think about their weight at all. Still others will wish that they had bigger breasts, while some may wish that their breasts were smaller. A number will dream of fame, money, and careers, while many more will simply hope for a home and food. Despite this diversity, whether they want to or not, all of these young women must make the transition from girl to woman.

Unfortunately, when a girl becomes a woman, she joins a disenfranchised group that does not receive equal pay and is still subject to discrimination throughout the world. Clitorectomies happen. Institutionalizing young women for suffering a "mental disorder" because they are gay happens. Forced prostitution happens. Discrimination in the workplace because a woman is having a family happens. These terrible injustices and more are a reality today, even though many adolescent women have not had the misfortune of dealing with inequity yet—and so doubt its existence. Young women must be careful not to complacently accept the inequality that does still exist in society today.

To live life on their own terms, young women will have to continue the force of change that was started by their mothers, grandmothers, and great-grandmothers. It is up to young women today to nurture and grow—and ultimately to pass along to the next generation—the gift of a woman's right to choose how she wants to live.

Hopefully, young women will continue to be proud of their femininity and all of the strength that it embodies. It would be the greatest gift to the next generation to break down the barriers of all kinds of discrimination so that women could be fully empowered in all that they choose to do. Someday, when all young women have equal opportunity to take control of their lives and dreams, then—and only then—will they truly become empowered.

Most importantly, collected here are images of adolescents that show us the faces of emerging women. They are a cross section that represents where young women today are and where they have been. Look at their faces and see women's history in the making. These adolescents are our past and present, and they hold our future and hopes in their hands.

Failing to remember our history, young women could inadvertently slip back to an outdated perception of their roles in the world that were created in a traditional patriarchal system. Young women need to mindfully guard the progress that women have already made and continue the process of gradual change to better the world in which we live.

Go forth into the world, young women. It belongs to you. Know yourself, maintain a healthy lifestyle, learn from your challenges, and rejoice in your blessings. Celebrate your womanhood and claim all of your power. You deserve to have the best in life.

46. A Yanamani Indian from Brazil adorns her face with sticks and leaves. (1989)
47. Girls wear ritual body paint outside a hut in Mandji, Gabon. (1984)

46

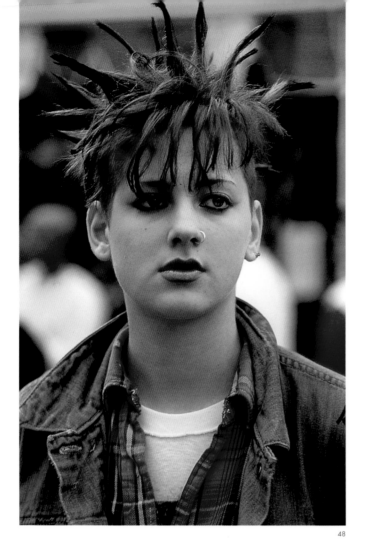

48. A young woman embodies the style of punk. (1985)
49. Properly attired, a young student learns verses from the Holy Book at the Timbuktu Koranic School in Mali. (1995)
50. A young woman attends the Woodstock Anniversary Festival in Woodstock, New York. (1994)

51

52

53

51. Nigerian young women wear jewelry and makeup. (1977)

52. One million teens gather for the Techno Love Parade at Tiergarten in Berlin, Germany. (1997)

53. Adolescent women wear special attire for a Chinese New Year's celebration in Singapore. (1985)

54. Islamic women have painted their faces in Tadjik, Dushambe, Russia. (1990)

55. Bari schoolgirls write in the sand in the Southern Sudani Equatoria Provence in Sudan. (1954)

56. Attired in the full Islamic hijab, only the eyes of one young woman may be seen while she attends a class at the Islamic College. (1991)

57. A cheerleader embraces a football player after a game. (1955)

56

58

58. Thirteen-year-old American wheelchair racer Leann Shannon takes the lead in the 200-meter dash
at the 1996 Paralympics in Atlanta, Georgia, USA. (1996)
59. Dancers perform in the first round of the Prix de Lausanne, a prestigious ballet competition in France. (1991)

60. A young African-American couple stands together in New York City. (1966)

61. At the Imilchil Bridal Market in Morocco, a young bride waits for a husband-to-be. (1984)

62. Fez newlywed wears the customary bridal ensemble for a frenetic day of wedding ceremonies in Morocco. (1995)

63. In Puerto Escondido, Oaxaca, Mexico, a couple lies together on the beach. (1992)

61

62

63

64

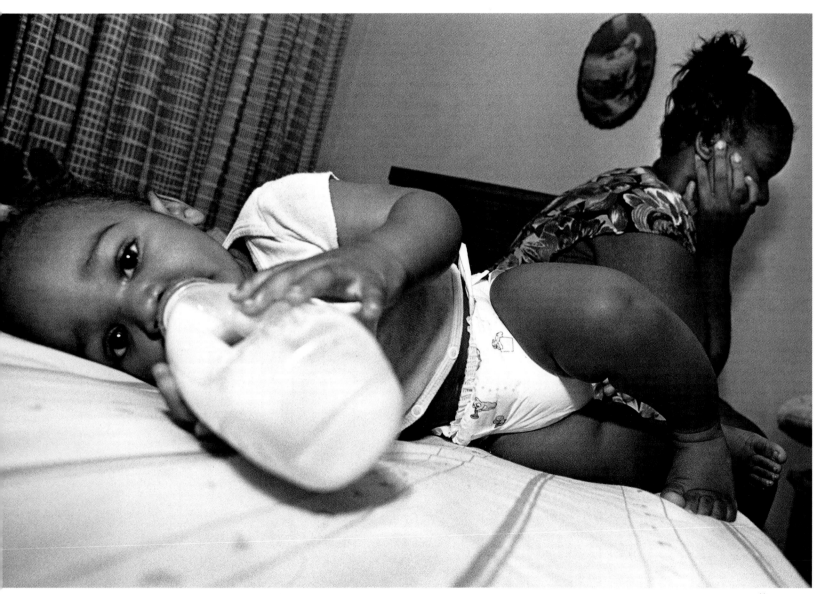

64. A seventeen year old holds her six-month-old baby in Seattle, Washington. (1994)

65. Fifteen-year-old "Ice" poses with her five-month-old son in Seattle, Washington. (1994)

66. An eighteen year old sits on the bed while her nine-month-old son drinks a bottle in Chicago, Illinois. (1994)

67

67. At the Selma March in Alabama, an African-American girl glares at a police officer with a confederate flag on his helmet. (1963)

68. "Julia" and other gang members spell out a sign for their gang—and the gun that "Julia" points is loaded in San Antonio, Texas. (1993)

69

70

69. In Tiananmen Square, China, a demonstrator holds up a red flag bearing a university's name. (1989)

70. A young woman carries a flag in protest in Prague, Czechoslovakia. (1989)

71. An anorexic teen has to be fed intravenously in the psychiatric department of the University of California–San Francisco Teaching Hospital. (1981)

72. A homeless girl sits on a curb in Los Angeles, California. (1992)
73. A young woman works in a field in Northern Bangladesh. (1983)
74. Young Peuhl women carry milk in calabashes in Timbuktu, Mali. (1988)

73

75

75. A young girl sits on a bed and knits in China. (1965)

76. College students hang out in the East Village, New York City. (1996)

77. A young gang member rides the subway in New York City. (1959)

76

womanhood

ESSAY BY WILMA MANKILLER

78. Two women pose for their portrait in Los Angeles, California. (1995)

WHEN I ASKED MYSELF, "What does it mean to be a woman in the 21st century? What special challenges will we face?", I realized that different women will have different responses to this question as race, culture, economic status, age, politics, and geography—as well as individual perspectives—will influence their answers.

Of course, the daily experiences of women vary greatly around the world. In Indonesia, the country with the world's largest Muslim population, women are questioning religious teachings about women and developing a new theology of women's rights based on reinterpreting the Koran. Women in India continue to face battery, sexual abuse—and even murder—in their own homes even though domestic abuse was made a crime in 1983. In Africa, a continent made up of 50 countries and 400 languages, women are reclaiming their history with an ambitious project entitled Women Writing Africa, an anthology which will include fiction, journals, songs, poems, historical documents, and letters. In the Iroquois Nations clan, mothers lead the struggle to maintain sovereignty rights which precede those of the United States government.

Collected in the following pages are images of women from around the world—women who are war refugees, housewives, athletes, farmers, factory workers, professional career women, and more. They are mothers, daughters, and sisters. They are friends, wives, and lovers. Most importantly, these women are part of the continuum of female experience. We share their laughter and sadness, their triumphs and failures. Most of all, we share their need to be autonomous while remaining connected to our heritages, to our families, and to our communities. To live life on our own terms, women have been—and must continue to be—unafraid to take risks and to stand up for what we believe in.

And so it is that women everywhere are working to create a world in which we hear the voices of women in politics, education, business, and every other sector of society. We hope to make this world a place where women and children are not raped or battered by men, where women have access to credit, health care, and education.

When contemplating the changes that need to be wrought, the Cherokee edict—"to be of good mind"—comes to me. It requires a holistic and spiritual approach—a belief that everything is interconnected. Women are connected to one another—and to men—through the societies in which we live. When we achieve gender equity for women, balance will be created between women and men—and only then will peace and harmony follow.

As women search for a societal model of gender equity, we may want to consider some indigenous societies. In Cherokee traditional culture, it was believed that the world existed in a precarious balance and that only right or correct actions maintained that balance. An important part of the balance was equity between men and women. Women were consulted in matters of importance to the community, the clan, the family, and the nation. When a man married a woman, he took up residence with the clan of his wife. We trace our clan ancestry through women. There was a women's council composed of women of each of the seven Cherokee clans. Female warriors called War Women or Pretty Women were tribal dignitaries. There was a belief that the Great Spirit sent messages through women. A woman's power was considered so great that special women were able to declare whether punishment or pardon was to be inflicted on those who offended the mandate to engage in only right or correct actions.

Equity between men and women was also evident in other tribal cultures such as: the Iroquois where women selected and had the right to depose male Chiefs; the Navajo where women controlled the economy by owning and managing the livestock; and the Ojibway women who trapped small animals, dressed furs, and built canoes. In some indigenous communities, women chose lives that transcended gender. Noted historian Connie Evans quotes a trader's observations about a Gros Ventres woman: "Although she dressed as a woman throughout her life, she pursued the role of a male in her adult years. . . . In time, she sat on the council and ranked as the third-leading warrior in a band of 180 lodges. . . . She took four wives. . . ."

If one puts our current global situation in an historical context, it is clear that women have made progress, though gains have been smaller for poor women and women of color. More women are leading business, political and educational institutions, and new laws protect women from violence, sexual harassment, and employment discrimination. In Sweden, Norway, Finland, Denmark, and Iceland, 39 percent of national legislative seats are held by women. In 1996, Peru created a women's rights ombudsman position to help eliminate widespread acceptance that some violence is a part of family life. In China, where boy babies were honored and girl babies once "disappeared," there is now a state family planning campaign proclaiming that girl babies are desired. It is important to recognize and appreciate the progress that we have made. It strengthens us—affirms us in who we are and empowers us to change the world in which we live.

Women will continue to extend a hand to one another, to meet, organize, and create change. Though change often occurs in very small increments, new forms of communication—the Internet, e-mail, wireless technology—may accelerate change as women in greater numbers network and share their stories of struggle and progress. And as women increasingly assume positions of power, we face a special challenge to resist models of unilateral leadership and use our new power in a liberating, collaborative way. We must help each other.

Author and activist Alice Walker coined the phrase "looking backward toward the future." As we contemplate the challenges women face this century, we can look back to a time when the voices of both women and men were honored and reconstruct a future in which women's rights are recognized as basic human rights—a future where economic exploitation of women is stopped and socially constructed limitations of a woman's rights are eliminated. In this future, women will define for themselves what it means to be a woman.

In the eighteenth century one of our Cherokee chiefs, astonished at the absence of women in delegations of colonial negotiators, asked, "Where are your women?" As we move forward into this century with faith, hope, and optimism, we must all ask that question again and again until the truthful answer can be "women are everywhere they want to be."

80

81

79. A woman is dressed for the National Festival of Folklore
    in the el Badia Palace grounds in Marrakech. (1986)

80. Garimpo Kayapas Indian women wear modern dress
    in Gorotire, Brazil. (1984)

81. A group of women wear native costume in Ghana. (1971)

82. A Nigerian woman has tribal scarring on her face. (1981)

82

83

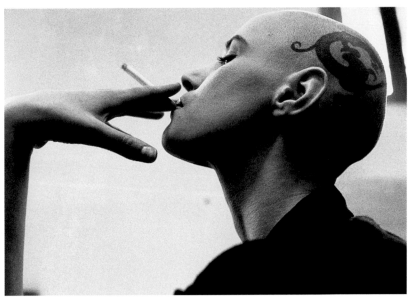

84

85

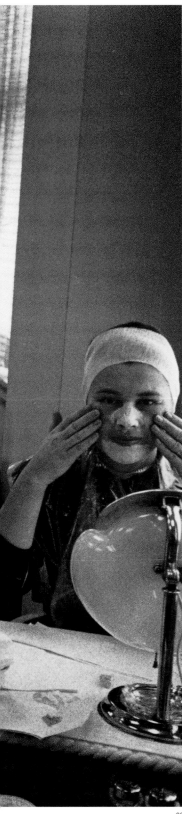

89

91. Contestants of the Miss Gibraltar Pageant go out dancing. (1995)
92. A woman gets a tattoo on Sunset Strip in Los Angeles, California. (1992)

91

92

93. Rain and mud do not dampen the spirits of this young woman in Woodstock, New York. (1994)

94. Couple from Kerala, India. (1987)
95. This couple flirts in the Spanish Governor's Palace in Old Havana, Cuba. (1994)
96. Lesbian lovers proclaim their love for one another in Houston, Texas. (1977)
97. Two students kiss at Oxford University, England. (1995)

95

96

97

98. A couple picks out an engagement ring. (1952)

99. At a bridal shop in Urumqi, China, brides try on both
    traditional Chinese and western wedding dresses. (1998)

100. A newly engaged couple kisses. (1952)

101. A bride and groom take wedding pictures on a hillside in Wales. (1965)

102. Bridesmaids pose for wedding photos in Harlem, New York City. (1962)

103. Lesbian wedding in London, England. (1968)

102

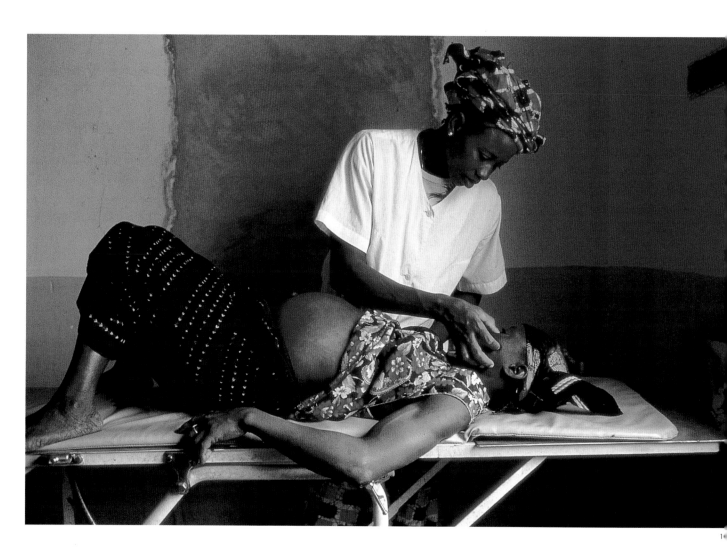

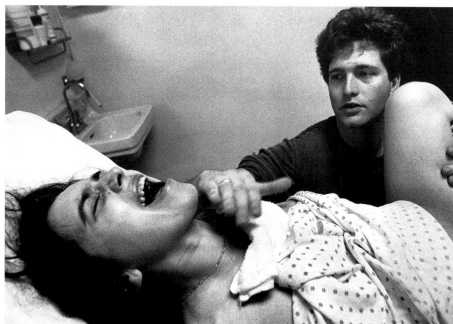

WOMANHOOD eighty-five

104. A clinician at a Catholic mission in Pel Dogon country in Mali attends to a pregnant woman. (1996)

105. A woman screams at the father when he tries to massage her shoulders during childbirth in Washington, D.C. (1990)

106. Mothers feed their babies in the Polizu Maternity Hospital in Bucharest, Rumania. (1989)

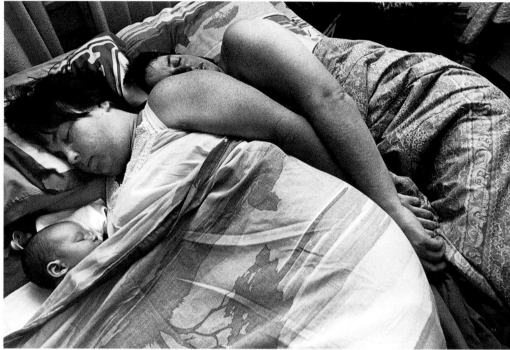

107.

107. Renee and Ann wanted to expand their family after "marrying." Gregg and Scott, who have been together for seven years, became the co-parents and the sperm donors. In July 1991, Connor was born and there began a loving, if controversial, family drama with the four parents questioning their relationships and responsibilities to the child and to each other. (1991)

108. A mother cooks and takes care of her children. (1950)

109

110

111

112

109. A woman and her son in the Kenilworth Apartment Projects in Washington, D.C. (1995)

110. A Tibetan mother carries her child in a sling on her back. (1985)

111. A mother cooks over an open fire while holding her child in Kinshasa, Zaire. (1995)

112. A woman hugs her baby. (1966)

113. While her son sleeps in her lap, a mother begs every night on the streets of San Francisco, California. (1991)
114. Fearing for their lives, the Touareg women fled Mali and have found shelter in the camps of the rebels in Adrar des Iforas. (1990)

114

115

115. In India, this woman was thrown out of her home by her new husband and his family because her dowry wasn't big enough—it didn't include a television and a motorcycle. (1987)

116. A woman mourns her husband who was killed in a land dispute in Oaxaca, Mexico. (1992)

117

118

119

117. At the funeral of her husband, President John Kennedy, Jacqueline Kennedy cradles the flag that draped his coffin in Arlington, Virginia. (1963)

118. A farewell service for late actor Danjuro held on November 13th at the Aoyama Funeral Hall in Tokyo. (1965)

119. These villagers honor the memory of men who are believed to have been murdered in Morelia, Mexico. (1994)

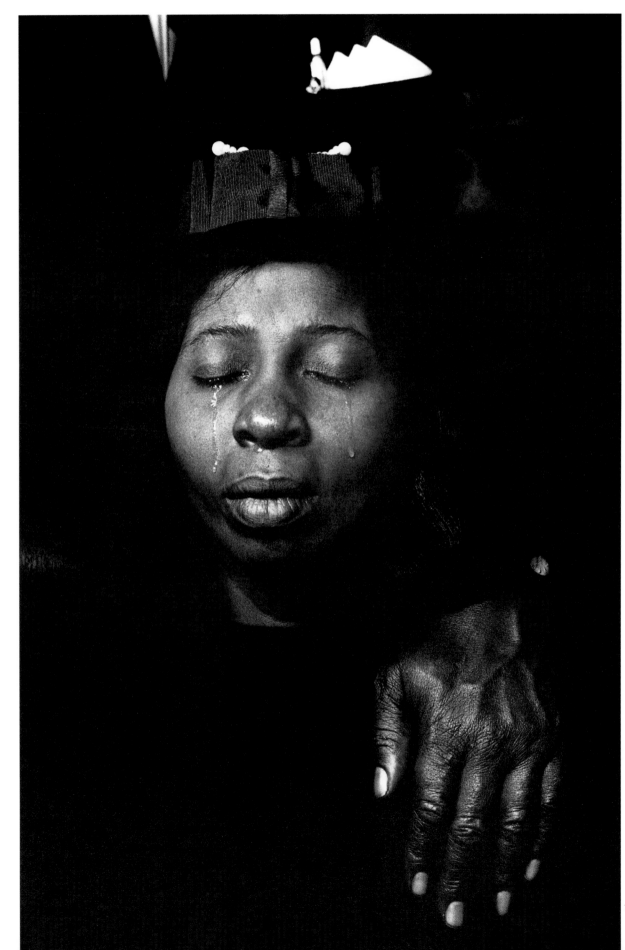

121

122

20. In South Carolina, an aunt cries at the funeral of her nephew who was killed in Vietnam. (1966)

21. This woman has returned from the United States to Ho Chi Minh City, Vietnam, to find her family. (1996)

22. In Arapai, Uganda, a woman looks at the charred ruins of her house which was burned down by raiders. (1986)

23. A female soldier from Indonesia. (1997)

125

124. Iran's chadored warriors are adept at handling pistols, rockets, automatic rifles, and more. Since Ayatollah Khomeini's 1982 appeal to the population
that it should form its own home guard, many women volunteered for service. (1986)
125. In an anti-Vietnam war protest, a woman holds a flower up to armed National Guardsmen in Washington, D.C. (1967)

126

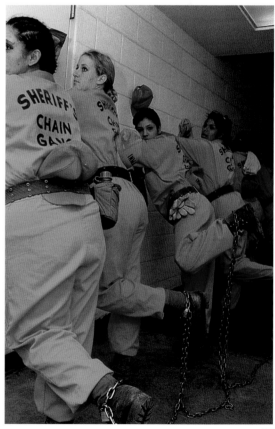

127

126. A Gestapo informer is recognized in a deportation camp in Dessau, Germany. (1944)

127. These prisoners wait for the chains to be removed so that they may return to their cells in Phoenix, Arizona. (1996)

128. These women are part of Africa's most famous "tribe," Nuba animists who live naked on the edge of the desert. The fundamentalist Khartoum government of General El-Bashir doesn't approve of their culture or religion and is trying to wipe them out by declaring a "holy war" in south Kurdofan. The Nuba face extinction. (1949)

129

129. A prostitute seduces a U.S. soldier in Seoul, South Korea. (1961)

130. A topless waitress serves drinks to a customer in California. (1965)

131. In Bombay, India, prostitutes await customers in a doorway on Foras Road. (1980)

133

134

132. A nurse clasps the hand of a woman undergoing an abortion in Oregon. (1985)

133. A member of Operation Rescue is arrested outside of an abortion clinic in Witchita, Kansas. (1991)

134. Women march at a pro-choice demonstration in Washington, D.C. (1989)

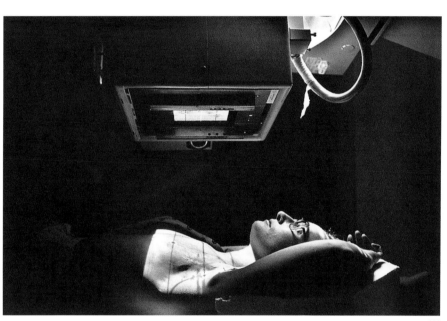

135

136

137

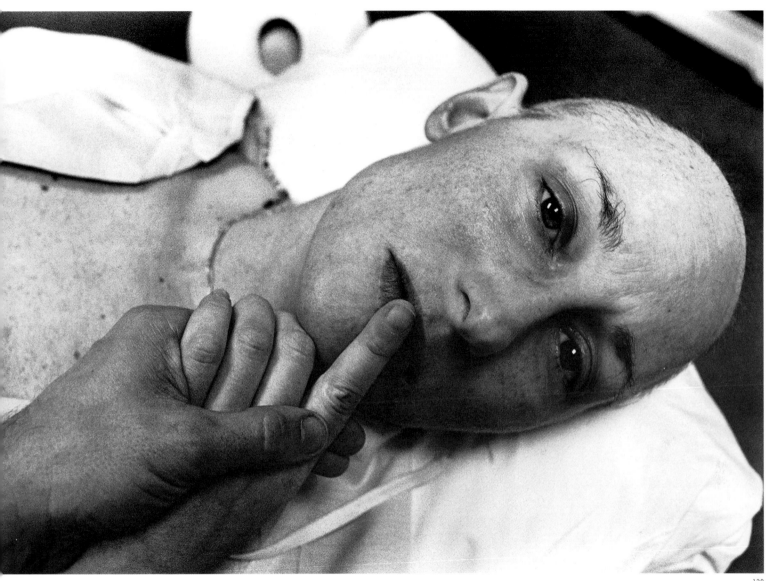

138

135. Dorothea's breast cancer is detected in Boston, Massachusetts. (1978)

136. After her mastectomy, Dorothea mourns the loss of her breast. (1978)

137. Nauseous from chemotherapy, Dorothea sits by the toilet. (1978)

138. In Boston Hospital, Dorothea loses her hair from chemotherapy. (1978)

139

140

139. Women pray at dawn at Srinagar in Kashmir, India. (1948)

140. In Tralee, Ireland, women form a religious procession. (1952)

141. Pilgrims watch the "holy waters" of Lake Pushkar, Rajasthan, India. (1975)
142. A candlelight ceremony is part of the Easter celebration in the Mixtec region of Oaxaca, Mexico. (1992)
143. In Varanasi, India, pilgrims pray and cleanse themselves in the Ganges River. (1981)

141

143

142

144

145

146

144. Protected by parasols, young women participate in the New Year's celebrations in China.

145. Before dancing in Taos, New Mexico, an aunt hugs her neice. (1993)

146. A woman participates in a Milumbu ritual dance at Kisannsani, Zaire. (1998)

147. While on a trek between Igli to Bab'n Ali, Berber women stop to do laundry in Djebel Sagrho, Morocco. (1994)
148. Med Star Trauma unit operates in Washington, D.C. (1991)
149. Members of Justice wear wigs during the annual Opening of Parliament ceremony in Freetown, West Africa. (1986)

147

149

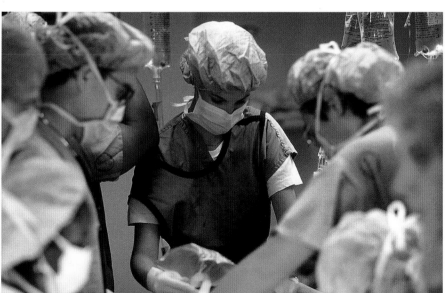

148

150. Woman lifeguard at Lake Michigan in Chicago. (1984)

151. Women officers participate in an African-American parade in Harlem, New York City. (1993)

152. This model/actress poses for a photo shoot. (1995)

153. At the Islamic Center of Ibn Taimiya, a teacher wears full chador and writes at the blackboard. (1995)
154. A music student practices violin in London, England. (1963)
155. A woman works in a Mormon cannery in Utah. (1971)
156. An artist paints in her studio. (1997)

154

153

155

156

157

158

157. Matador Mari Paz Vega waves a red cape to incite the charging bull
in Caceres bullring at Torremolinos, Spain. (1997)

158. All-female crew from Christ Church races others during an eight-week regatta
at Oxford University, England. (1998)

159. U.S. Women's Soccer Team practices in San Diego, California. (1998)

159

160

161

160. Women cyclists train in Tehran, Iran. (1998)
161. Boxer Kate Sekules trains at Gleason's Gym in New York City. (1997)

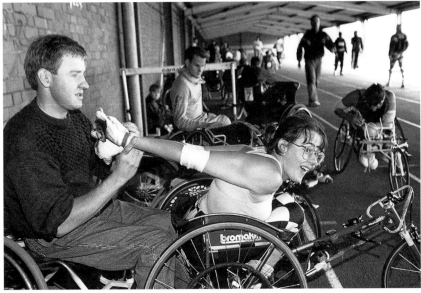

163

162. A woman competes in the javelin throw at the Paralympics in Barcelona, Spain. (1992)

163. Ian Thompson and Tanni Grey warm up before a wheelchair race at the Paralympics in Barcelona, Spain. (1992)

166

165. A grandmother holds her sleeping grandchild. (1995)

166. An elderly couple hugs on the street. (1966)

167. A grandmother kisses her yawning grandchild on the cheek. (1988)

168

168. A woman's hand is kissed in the main square in Kracow, Poland. (1964)
169. An elderly couple lounges in bed in Germany. (1981)

170. In the washroom of the Metropolitan Opera House, a woman primps during intermission in New York City. (1950)

171. A woman poses for a portrait in El Salvador. (1983)

172

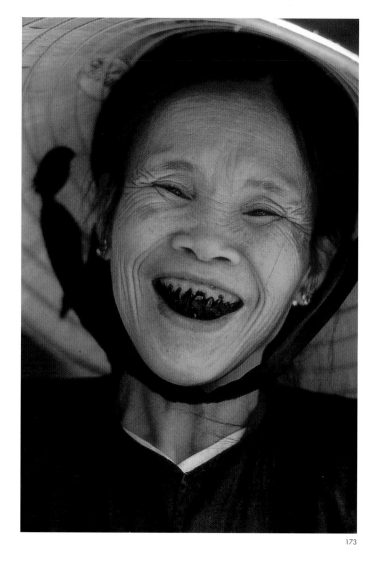

173

174

172. An elderly woman smiles mysteriously in China. (1995)

173. A woman laughs in Vietnam. (1989)

174. In Cubotao, Brazil, a woman takes a break. (1995)

175. A woman closes her eyes for a moment in Hong Kong. (1959)

176

177

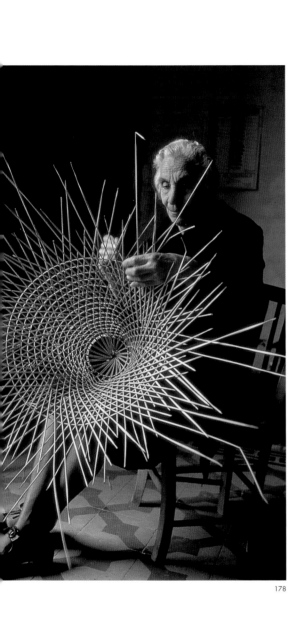

178

179

176. A tourist has her picture taken in New Zealand. (1989)

177. A Bakubung ba Ratheo tribe member hangs laundry in Transvaal province, South Africa. (1994)

178. A weaver makes a trap to catch fish in Sicily, Italy. (1975)

179. Women wear neck rings in Burma. (1977)

181

180. An elderly woman prepares herring for a customer on Hester Street in New York City. (1950)
181. A woman sells tickets in a movie theater. (1972)
182. An astrologer plays keyboard on a pier in Key West, Florida, to draw customers. (1989)

183. A secretary types while bank executives have a meeting in Dallas, Texas. (1965)
184. Cinda Hallman, DuPont's Chief Information Officer, won *Information Week Magazine*'s "Top CIO of 1995." (1995)

183

185

186

187

185. Reverend Katherine Young at St. Paul's in Northern Ireland was the first woman to be ordained priest by the Anglican Church. (1997)
186. At an old-age home in Ivry-sur-Seine, France, a resident gets playful. (1975)
187. Seventy-four-year-old Maria Pignatelli visits and comforts the elderly and sick in La Boca, Buenos Aires. (1993)
188. An elderly woman sits quietly in Trinidad, Cuba. (1994)

190

189. Seventy-eight-year-old Madeleine Lacombe resides in a small stone cottage without running water in Aubas, France;
    she lives off her land, her poultry, and her fruit trees—and cannot afford shopping and luxuries. (1987)
190. Gail, a homeless woman, lives on the street with all of her possessions in San Francisco, California. (1992)

191

192

193

191. An elderly lady refuses to leave the ruined city of Chechyna, Grozny. (1995)

192. Women pray on a road, facing Russian soldiers, to stop their advance during the Chechyna War. (1994)

193. Elderly women demonstrate in the National March for Women's Lives in Washington, D.C. (1986)

195

196

194. A woman crosses the finish line in the track-and-field event of the Sun City Senior Olympics in Sun City, Arizona. (1979)

195. This fencing mistress teaches class at Wycombe Abbey, Buckinghamshire, England. (1963)

196. The Sun City cheerleader squad practices a routine in Sun City, Arizona. (1979)

197. Friends enjoy a snack on the grass in front of the Statue of Liberty in New York City. (1970)

198. Elderly women judge a naked man dancing in front of them in Bakersfield, California. (1983)

199. Women sit on a park bench and talk. (1975)

197

198

199

200

200. Two elderly women sit on a low wall in Paris, France, drinking from a thermos. (1995)